Rhyd-y-ca
A Welsh Mining Community

The life, death and re-creation of a Welsh mining community, 1800-1980

By Eurwyn Wiliam

Rhyd-y-car from the nearby tip, 1980. The houses re-erected at the Museum of Welsh Life are the last six in the front row. Note the pigeon-lofts and living-sheds in the gardens

Preface

For the past three thousand years, iron has played a central role in man's development and has made possible the creation of an urban, industrialised society.

The perfection of a means of mass-producing iron during the late eighteenth century laid the foundations for the Industrial Revolution, and the little township of Merthyr Tudful found itself at the centre of this development. The three essential ingredients necessary for iron production were iron ore (which, when melted at high temperature, produced iron), timber (for making charcoal for the smelting furnaces) and water (for driving the water wheels which operated the bellows for the furnaces). All three were to be found in Merthyr, and by the end of the nineteenth century the area had been transformed into one of the most heavily industrialised parts of Britain.

In December 1979 a disastrous flood finally sealed the fate of a historic community on the outskirts of Merthyr. The twenty-nine houses at Rhyd-y-car had been built by Richard Crawshay in about 1800 as homes for his iron workers, and the inhabitants of the two terraces were indissolubly linked firstly with the iron and then with the coal industry. By 1980 however, Rhyd-y-car presented a sad sight. The houses, condemned in the mid-1930s, had mostly been bought by the Borough Council who had resettled their inhabitants, though a few lingered on. Most of the houses were boarded up, but now and then thieves would break in and steal anything of value that remained: the floor boards, the joists and the stone flags from the ground floors were in many cases removed along with the roof slates. The once-immaculate gardens were overgrown, half-hiding the numerous sheds, coal-houses and privies. Goats

Re-erection work in progress

perched on the corrugated-iron roofs, dogs and bedraggled horses wandered everywhere. But it had not always been so, as this book will show.

When Merthyr Tudful Borough Council offered some of the Rhyd-y-car houses to the Museum of Welsh Life for re-erection, we were able to begin a project that was unique in Britain, and probably in Europe. Other museums have furnished terraces of houses in order to show how their interiors changed with time, but none have chosen to show the changes made to a building's fabric over nearly two centuries. There are two over-riding educational advantages to such a method: firstly, it shows that culture is not static, which can be an impression in folk and open-air museums where all buildings and their contents tend to look alike over long periods of time; and secondly, by bringing the story up to the present we can provide a key to the past with which all can identify. History began yesterday. For this reason we have chosen to extend the story beyond 1980, and have shown the last house as it would have been changed had the site not been condemned and finally demolished some years earlier.

The entire re-erection and reconstruction is based on extensive research – architectural, documentary and oral – and no value judgements are meant or implied. We have tried to record what actually happened in the past and what happens today, and it should not be taken that the changes carried out to some of these houses necessarily carry a Museum of Welsh Life 'seal of approval'. Through the re-erected houses and the voices of the former inhabitants recorded in this book and the associated cassette, we hope to have recorded something of the vibrant life of a historic Welsh mining community.

Merthyr and Rhyd-y-car

What happened in south Wales in the eighteenth century was to transform the history of the world. Ironstone occurred naturally in the area now known as the Heads of the Valleys, and there were ample woodlands to be converted into charcoal with which to smelt it and later coal to the same end.

This happy coincidence brought to the area the great English ironmasters, the Guests, Bacons, Crawshays, Homfrays and Hills, seeking further fortunes, and in the process turning the villages and small towns of Blaenafon, Beaufort, Sirhywi, Hirwaun, Aberdare and Merthyr into world leaders in the production of iron and the mining of coal. The Dowlais furnaces were opened in 1759, the Plymouth Works in 1763, Cyfarthfa two years later and Penydarren in 1784. Their output was largely pig-iron, carried down to Cardiff on horseback. In 1794 however the marketing situation was dramatically improved with the building of the Glamorganshire Canal which ran from Richard Crawshay's Cyfarthfa plant to Cardiff.

The new canal was spanned by iron bridges, one of which is now restored and re-located outside Chapel Row, Georgetown. Richard Crawshay bought most of the land on the west bank of the river Taff including Rhyd-y-car farm. On the land between the canal and Nant Cwm-y-glo, next to the iron bridge, he began to build houses for the miners of the Rhyd-y-car iron-ore mine which supplied his Ynys-fach iron works, opened in 1801. Two rows of the houses were erected at right

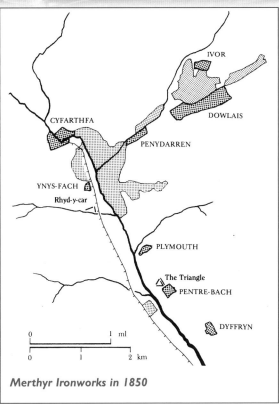

Merthyr Ironworks in 1850

angles to each other in three stages. The first six are the ones now re-erected at the Museum. They were followed by a row of sixteen houses at right angles to these (which are shown on a map of 1814). Finally, seven houses were added to the south end of the first six in about 1815, at a slightly different alignment, caused by a curve in the canal.

The houses were all of a particular type associated with the Crawshay family. The main structure consisted of two storeys with a single room on each floor, 4m by 3.8m in size, with a small single extension to the back where there was a pantry and the main bedroom built under a continuation of the roof. The Rhyd-y-car houses were all built as mirror-image pairs, so that the last house in the row had its fire place and chimney-stack in the gable while it was separated by a thin timber-and-brick partition from the next house. That in turn had its fireplace backing on to that of the third house, so that there was a double-thickness fireplace wall and double chimney stack every two houses. The stacks were also of brick though the houses themselves were built of stone. The roofs were of local stone tiles (in a few years it would become cheaper to transport Caernarfon slates by sea to Cardiff and thence to Merthyr on the canal than it would be to transport stone tiles by pack-animal from ten miles away). Circular stairs located in the thickness of the fireplace gable led to the loft: in these houses they are timber, though the company reverted to the tried and trusted traditional stone staircases in the remaining houses at Rhyd-y-car.

Nos 17-29 Rhyd-y-car in 1980. Notice the change in alignment which occurs after no. 22

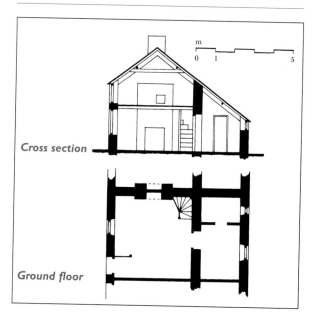

m
0 1   5

Cross section

Ground floor

Nearly 400 such houses are known to have existed in the valleys, most, if not all, connected in some way with the various Crawshay ironworks at Merthyr, Aberdare, Hirwaun, and Rhymney and the associated Bailey works at Nantyglo. The Rhyd-y-car houses are the smallest of all the examples built in the area in the period 1795-1830, and so represent the minimum standard acceptable to the relatively enlightened Crawshay family. The houses had to be good enough to attract workers to serve the company, for many dwellings in Merthyr were of extremely poor quality, as B.H. Malkin noted in 1807:

> The first houses were only very small and simple cottages for furnace-men, forge-men, miners and such tradesmen as were necessary, built in scattered confusion, without any order or plan. As the works increased more cottages were erected in the spaces between ... so as to form ... irregular streets ... very filthy for the most part and doubtless very unhealthy.

At that time, however,

> ... Mr Crawshay's ironworks at Cyfarthfa are by far the largest in Europe, and in that case, as far as we know, the largest in the world. He employs constantly fifteen hundred men, at an average of thirty shillings per week per man, which will make the weekly wages paid by him two thousand, two hundred and fifty pounds, and the monthly expenditure, including other items, about ten thousand pounds.

Ironstone was a primary raw material required by the huge melting furnaces. A dramatic rise in the demand for iron during the late eighteenth and early nineteenth centuries (during and following the Napoleonic Wars) led to an expansion of iron production in Merthyr and by 1800 Richard Crawshay decided to concentrate local production near the source of the ironstone itself (the Rhyd-y-car mine) at Ynys-fach, about a mile south of Cyfarthfa, with new furnaces being built there in 1801. Men and women alike worked in the ironworks: in 1850 over 600 women laboured in the Merthyr ironworks. They were employed as 'pollers' who unloaded the ore from the trams and piled it ready for the furnaces, 'ironstone girls' who broke up large lumps of ironstone for smelting, 'coke girls' who stacked coking coal,

A reason for existence: Thomas Hornor's view of the Cyfartha rolling mills c.1817. The Rhyd-y-car houses were built for the workers who supplied Cyfarthfa's sister works, Ynys-fach, with its raw material, iron ore

'brickyard girls', 'tippers' who helped clear the cinder trams, and 'pilers' who piled and weighed the iron: three pilers were expected to pile thirty-five tons of hot iron a day between them. Until 1842, women and children commonly worked underground, both in the ironstone mines and in the coal mines which were beginning to replace coke as the main fuel. Elizabeth Williams aged ten, and sisters Mary and Rachel Enoch, aged eleven and twelve, worked in one of the Dowlias company's coal mines:

> We are door-keepers in the four-foot level. We leave the house before six each morning and are in the level until seven o'clock and sometimes later. We get 2d. a day and our light costs us 21/2d. a week. Rachel was in a day school and she can read a little. She was run over by a tram a while ago and was home ill a long time, but she has got over it.

The houses that these children and other workers lived in were often poor, as noted in a report of 1850:

The first impression of a stranger who visits Merthyr is that it is a town of workmen's houses … The style of building is of the rudest and most commodious kind … There still exist several of the original houses, mere hovels of stone, having no upper storey, and covered with thatch, the eaves of which may be touched with the hand. On this type the builders have improved, by the addition of a loft above the ground floor, and in many instances by a division of the dwelling into four rooms; but as if alarmed by this innovation, they have done this timidly and scantily, for the houses are still very low and ill-ventilated. The better class of tradesmen have advanced a little, raising their houses to the second floor, but in a narrow spirit, for the upper rooms cannot but be inconveniently low … There is not a public sewer or drain throughout the town of Merthyr — a place be it remembered having upward of 40,000 inhabitants … The houses … have no privies, nor any receptacle whatsoever for household refuse. The consequences, as regards public decency and health, are absolutely shocking.

Merthyr Tudful High Street c. 1850

Prior to the census returns of 1841 very little detailed information is available regarding the employment of the workers who lived at Rhyd-y-car or indeed of the total number of persons who lived there. A retrospective view based on the census returns of 1841 and 1851 coupled with the location next to the iron-ore mine nevertheless suggests that almost all of the first working occupants would have been employed as ironstone miners or in some other related occupation. The ironstone miners were the cream of the Merthyr working-class, being the only workers in the town able to afford gold watches. Many of them were originally immigrants to the new boom town; the vast majority of them were from Glamorgan but others were from west and mid Wales. In 1840, only nine per cent of the town's population was not Welsh, and Welsh was its daily language. The Rhyd-y-car houses were of good quality compared to many in Merthyr and were certainly a vast improvement on the farmworkers' cottages that many of the first inhabitants had been used to. Lack of ventilation and no toilets would have been nothing new to them; they had chosen to come to Merthyr and earn wages unheard-of in the countryside.

By 1841, sixty-nine per cent of Rhyd-y-car's working population of seventy were still employed as ironstone miners, with a further five (seven per cent) working as hauliers. Hauliers too were at the very top of the working-class, being self-employed men who owned their own horses. Lewsyn yr Heliwr, one of the main leaders of the Merthyr Rising of 1831 when Crawshay's workers fought pitched battles with the army, was one of these men. At least three boys aged twelve or under living in Rhyd-y-car were employed as miners, and two girls worked as labourers. In 1801 Merthyr had a population of 7,000 and was the largest town in Wales; it remained so for sixty years, overshadowing Swansea and the large village of Cardiff. By 1831 it had a population of 30,000, increasing at rate of fifty per cent every ten years. Even with the primitive sanitation, the death rate was no worse than that of any small country town, but there was a great difference in how long working-class babies would live compared to middle-class ones. Three-quarters of all who died in Merthyr were children under five, but those who survived had a chance of outliving their country cousins. Religion flourished, with a new chapel being built every year. Independents and Baptists were the commonest denominations, followed by the Methodists.

Eleven per cent of Rhyd-y-car's working population were coal-miners in 1841. In spite of the enthusiastic expansion programmes at Cyfarthfa and Ynys-fach during the 1830s and 1840s, it was becoming apparent by 1850 that the Crawshay iron boom was past its peak and in that year ironstone had to be imported from as far afield as Whitehaven in Cumbria in order to maintain production at Cyfarthfa. This is in part reflected in the census returns for Rhyd-y-car in 1851 by which time the number of iron miners had dropped to thirty-four and forty per cent of the total working population, from sixty-nine per cent ten years earlier.

Coal mining on the other hand accounted for eighteen people, an increase of fourteen per cent on the 1841 figures. The number in associated trades such as hauliers and tippers stood at ten.

Because of inadequate sanitation and over-crowding, cholera struck the town in 1849, and 470 people died in the lower part of the town. A further 962 died in upper Merthyr which included Penydarren and Dowlais. Five years later cholera struck again, killing 424 people. Five people died of cholera at Rhyd-y-car in 1849 and one in 1854. Typhus was also endemic. As a result of these deaths several inquiries were commissioned to look into the causes of the outbreaks and to suggest ways of improving conditions. These reports include detailed

Cholera at Merthyr-Tydfil.

RETURN OF CASES,
TUESDAY, JULY 31, 1849.

MERTHYR.	ATTACKED.	DEAD.
Total from commencement (May 25th), as per last Report, corrected by Registration Returns up to 10 A.M., Yesterday	1415	593
New Cases, up to 10 A.M., To-day	18	12
DOWLAIS.		
Total from commencement (June 10th), up to 10 A.M, Yesterday	536	231
New Cases, up to 10 A.M., To-day	23	8
ABERDARE.		
Total from commencement (June 24th), up to 10 A.M, Yesterday	211	36
New Cases, up to 10 A.M., To-day	8	4
TOTAL	2211	884

FRANK JAMES,
Clerk to the Guardians.

H. W. WHITE, PRINTER, MERTHYR.

A house interior at Cefncoedycymmer, Merthyr, in the closing decades of the nineteenth century. Although the furnishings are very similar, the house obviously considerably larger than the ones at Rhyd-y-car

comments on the housing situation. William Kay's report of 1854 notes how

> Comparatively few – in fact, scarcely any – of the windows allow of being opened at the top, and from their generally small size, admit a very inadequate portion of light; whilst some are … fixtures

Kay also noted that the houses were generally well kept:

> With rare exceptions the interiors of the cottages of the Welsh – your own countrymen and women – are distinguished by extreme cleanliness, well ordered arrangements, furniture, which is obviously their pride, and scrupulous neatness and propriety.

The anonymous correspondent of the *The Morning Chronicle* published detailed notes on the contents of the houses of Merthyr in 1849-51:

> The houses of the workmen are built in rows of uniform height and size. They are of three classes. The best are of two stories, have four small sash windows (which, by the way, are never opened), two above and one on each side the door. On the ground floor there is a roomy kitchen with a stone floor; adjoining is a small room, just large enough to contain a four-post bed, a chest of drawers, a small corner cupboard, two chairs, a window table, which usually form its contents. The ceiling is not plastered, and the rafters are used for hanging up the crockery and the household utensils. Above

stairs are two bedrooms, one large and the other small; the ceiling here is of lath and plaster. This is all, except, perhaps a narrow cupboard cut off from the lower bedroom, and dignified with the name of 'pantry'. There is no strip of garden, no backdoor or outlet, no place of accommodation, no drain to carry away house refuse, nor any pump or pipe for the supply of water. The street in front is consequently made the receptacle of every kind of abomination conceivable.

Such are the residences of the best class of workmen in and around Merthyr. These houses are, for the most part, the very type of cleanliness and order. They are stuffed with furniture even to superfluity; a fine mahogany eight-day clock, a showy mahogany chest of drawers, a set of mahogany chairs with solid seats, a glass-fronted cupboard for the display of china, glass and silver spoons, forming indispensable requisites for the principal room. The other apartments are equally well furnished. The habits of the women with respect of their houses, are those of cleanliness, decency, and order. They are always scrubbing the rooms, polishing and regulating the furniture, or with long brushes are laying white or yellow washes upon the front of their houses. In short, the people themselves do their duty; but there being no town authorities to look to cleansing, draining and scavenging, the streets are in a state of disgusting filth, abounding in fermenting and putrefying substances, equally offensive to decency and injurious to public health. For such a house the workman pays from 10s to 13s a month. The

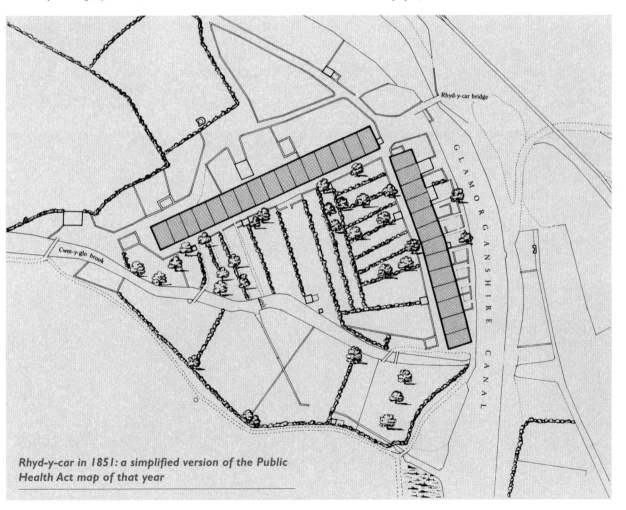

Rhyd-y-car in 1851: a simplified version of the Public Health Act map of that year

second-class houses have but two rooms, one above stairs and one below; for these, the rents vary from 6s to 8s a month. There are third-class houses having only one room, for which the rent is about 4s a month.

The correspondent continued:

In support of what I have above said of the furnishing of the cottages and the condition of the inmates, I will give the particulars I observed in two or three houses belonging to different classes of the workmen.

Cyfarthfa Row. This was one of the roomiest and best cottages I had seen in the ironworks. It was new. It had a fine large kitchen, a good parlour, a convenient pantry with a window, and 2 lofty-ceilinged bedrooms upstairs. There was a small strip of garden behind, and (mirabile dictu!) a privy at command; there was one to every six houses in the row. Nevertheless the rent was only 8s a month. In this case there was evidently a diminution of rent in consideration of services. The house was literally crammed with furniture. In the kitchen were two mahogany chests of drawers, each of which supported a looking-glass, tea-tray, a bread-basket, tea-caddies and some books amongst which I observed Burhitt on the New Testament ... and Bagsters' Comprehensive Bible. There was also a well-polished eight-day clock, and a set of good mahogany chairs. On the walls were a quantity of print in gold frames. Between 2 pieces of needlework was a portrait of Our Saviour upon one of the walls. Another has a good looking-glass, a coloured portrait of the Duke of Wellington, and a large print of the Battle of Waterloo. From the rafters of the floor above hung a canary bird in his cage, a lanthorn, and a quantity of jugs enough to have supplied a harvest- home supper. Over the fireplace there was displayed a bottle-jack, and small bellows, Italian iron and flat-irons, extra tongs, poker and shovel, and a variety of useful little articles, all kept bright as silver. The window was filled with a large myrtle. (Here I may remark upon the habit of cultivating flowers indoors, which is universal amongst the labouring classes. I have seen everywhere an abundance of arums, geranium, cinerarias, myrtles, and the like, which

thrive most luxuriantly, owing I presume, to the warmth of their apartments, which have always a large blazing fire.) In the parlour there was a good four-post bedstead, a French-polished chest of drawers, covered with a profusion of glass and other articles, including a cruet stand and decanters, with small figures of the Queen and Prince Albert in china-ware, a neat work-box, and some ornamental shells. In a corner was a glass-fronted cupboard, filled with china and glass, and displaying ostentatiously silver sugar tongs and a set of spoons. There was also a mahogany table with a bright copper tea-kettle reposing on it. On the walls were framed prints of St. John and St. Luke, with a portrait of King George IV between them. Behind the door hung a quantity of male and female wearing apparel, and beside it were some shelves loaded with books amongst which were Bunyan's 'Pilgrim's Progress', the 'Complete Works of Flavius Josephus' (in Welsh) , 'Haver Bedyddwyr' (History of the Baptists), M'Donalds 'Family Cook',

The Rhyd-y-car children attended Cae-draw Primary School. This is the Infants class of 1919.

'The Evangelical Rambler', a Welsh Bible, 'Cydymarth-y-bibl' (Bible-class book), and an English 'Book of Common Prayer'. A slate, a hat, a bonnet, and pair of child's boots, completed the inventory of this room. The apartments upstairs were equally well furnished. They had four-post and a stump bedstead, mahogany chairs and tables, looking-glasses, coffers for keeping clothes, a pair of scales for weighing flour, a spinning wheel and other conveniences. The floor-boards were as white as snow, and all furniture was polished and kept with great care.

I should state that in selecting that house I took the first that I met with, where the furniture appeared remarkably good. I next took an average second-class house. It was inhabited by a collier working at Pen-y-darran; and though it had but 2 small rooms, the rent was the same as that of the last house, namely 8s a month. The wife kept a small huckster's shop – a common practice hereabouts. She sold apples, gingerbread, herrings, bacon, and a few other articles which did not require a license. In reply to my questions, she said, "My husband is at Pen-y-darran; he earns about 10s a week; sometimes he gets 11s, but never more. My mother died in this house of cholera." I was amused with some odd-looking characters in chalk on a cupboard-door. She told me she could not write, but nevertheless could keep accounts, and she did so readily. I cannot pretend to describe the marks she had for names, but the notation of a shilling was expressed by a ring, that of sixpence by a circle with a spike issuing from the centre, and horizontal lines a halfpenny. Among the furniture of this house I noticed one chest of drawers, on which stood a tea-tray, two waiters, and a few books, including a bible, the 'Young Woman's Companion', the 'Popular Story Teller', etc. On the books were a clothes and hair brush; and hanging on the wall above, was a small looking-glass. One round and one square deal table, 3 chairs, a wicker cradle, a Dutch clock without a case, and a few useful articles over the fireplace, consisting of brass candlesticks, a coffeepot, and the like, constituted the whole of the furniture of this room. In a small back window there hung a canary in his cage, and a flower, which the good woman informed me was 'nettle geranium'. There was an infant in the cradle only 3 months old. A few small *pictures decorated the walls; among them was a tribute of affection to the memory of the woman's little brother – it was a coloured French lithograph, cleverly executed, of a child reclining his head upon his hands. It had been bought from a fancied resemblance to the deceased brother.*

Following the cholera outbreaks of 1849 and 1854 and the subsequent inquiries, improvements were carried out to the houses of Merthyr. The fixed windows were replaced by opening sash or casement windows, piped water was provided to standpipes located near terraces and the first planned drainage systems were installed. Later, earth closets shared between two houses were built in the front gardens. Three communal baking ovens were also built at the end of the rows. In 1851, almost seventy per cent of the occupants of Rhyd-y-car had been born locally, nearly a third of them in the two streets themselves. 169 people lived in the twenty-nine houses on the day of the census, 124 of them being permanent residents, seventeen visiting relatives and twenty-eight lodgers. The iron boom was largely over and the population growth was slowing down. The sinking of coal mines elsewhere meant that places like Aberdare were now beginning to grow rapidly and to compete with Merthyr which had been hit hard both by this slump and by the cholera epidemics.

The 1861 census shows a pattern of employment in Rhyd-y-car virtually unchanged from that of 1851, ironstone mines accounting for thirty-seven workers and the coal mine eighteen; the number of hauliers stood at six but the number of ordinary labourers had dropped form five to one. There was a small increase in craftsmen, with two smiths and two engineers being noted on the returns. Between 1861 and 1871, however, there was a marked drop in the population from 169 to 131, a drop that was reflected in the total male working population from sixty-six (in 1861) to forty-one. This can be attributed in part at least to the increasing age of the population, with many of the older members of the families and extended families (in-laws and grandparents) having presumably died in the meantime. But more significantly is the fact that for the first time the people employed in the coal mines (fifteen) exceeded those working in the ironstone mines (thirteen), with a further nine people described as hauliers, though whether in the ironstone or coal mines is not specified.

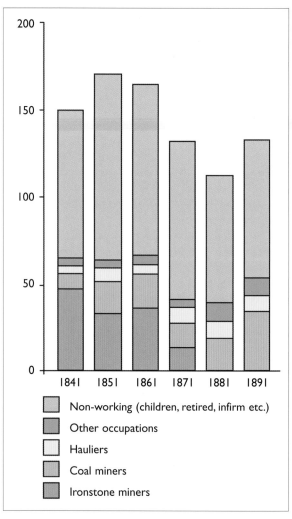

Occupations in Rhyd-y-car, 1841-91, based on the census returns

In 1881 there were thirty-eight working males at Rhyd-y-car, almost half the number found there in 1841, 1851 and 1861; an average of over two working men (wage earners) per dwelling between 1841 and 1861 had dropped to just over one per house. Several dwellings were in the names of women occupants, possibly through the death of a husband from cholera or accident at work. Of the working male population nineteen (or half) were coal miners, ten were hauliers and four were labourers. There were no ironstone miners, and only two hauliers and one labourer were described as being associated with the ironstone operations. This confirms the trend since 1841 of a steady decline in emphasis on ironstone mining and rise in the importance of coal over the same period.

Ten years later (1891) the population of the terraces numbered 137, the majority of the working males being employed in the coal industry. Thirty-four were recorded as coal miners, one as a coal weigher and eight as hauliers. One man is described as a stoker and another two worked an engine (presumably a steam engine), though whether these were associated with the coal mines or iron works or the railway is not specified. Most of the womenfolk spent their time looking after the home, though a few did have outside jobs. Janet Evans, a widow aged seventy-two, and living on her own in no. 8 earned her rent money as a laundress, whilst the eighteen-year old daughter of William and Mary Graves in house no.11 was a dressmaker, as was Mary Jones in no. 27. Elizabeth Williams, who lived with her brother Thomas, was described as a 'Hawker' and probably went around from house to house selling her wares. Two other, unmarried, girls worked as maids or housekeepers in the larger houses in Merthyr.

By 1891 these houses were already considered out-dated and cramped, and yet there was reluctance to move away to newer, more spacious accommodation. It is perhaps surprising to note that fourteen of the twenty-six houses that were inhabited in that year had five or more occupants, with no fewer than ten of these having seven or more. In fact house no. 14 boasted ten occupants, namely, Thomas and Ellen Morgan, the latter aged fifty, and their eight children whose aged ranged from three to twenty-one. A similar picture was found in no. 26 where John Jones lived with his daughter and son-in-law and their eight children.

Most of the Rhyd-y-car menfolk continued to be employed in the coal mines until the 1960s. This long period saw many fluctuations. Unemployment in Merthyr was only 1.4 per cent in 1913 but the world-wide economic slump of 1926 hit the area particularly hard, for the original benefits of Merthyr's location now meant that it was far from both its raw materials and its markets. Three thousand steelworkers lost their jobs in 1930: 12,000 jobs were lost between 1921 and 1931, and 17,000 left the town in the same decade followed by a further 10,000 up to 1939. The human cost of this was summarised by the correspondent of The Times in 1928:

The effects of two or three years without work on a man and his family are worth thinking over. He will have been receiving unemployment benefit, 23s. a week for husband and wife, and 2s. for each child. He will scarcely have been paying less than 6s.6d. a week in rent for two rooms. If he is unfortunate in his dwellings, the second room may be an unventilated cellar, for in some parts under-houses were built on that system into the hillside. Otherwise, the actual houses are mostly satisfactory, but past prosperity has left high rents as its legacy. Still a family of five can be kept in food on 22s.6d., if that were all the story. It is not. Debts were contracted in 1926, the summer and autumn that swallowed up all previous savings … As the months go by, first boots and clothing wear out and then bedclothes and cooking utensils (but) these out-of-work miners are not slum dwellers. They are cultivated people, with self-respect and an obvious pride in home cleanliness and sparkling brasses on the chimney piece …

These same years saw most of the Rhyd-y-car houses sold by the Crawshay family and bought by a local entrepreneur, who then offered the houses for resale after partly re-roofing them with slates instead of the existing stone tiles. As the houses had been condemned as unfit for habitation many inhabitants did not buy, preferring to continue to pay rent. Those that bought paid some £50 to £55 with payments spread over four or five years. The Second World War brought fuller employment, with factories owned by Unilever, Rotax and ICI being set up. The post-war slump was answered by a government initiative, and companies such as Teddington Aircraft Controls (1945-71), Lines Bros/Triang (1946-83), BSA (1951-58), Thorn Electrical Industries (1951-), O.P. Chocolates and Hoover (1951-) brought wider employment opportunities for women as well as men. The 1970s and 1980s again saw depression hitting the old industrial communities, although this time accompanied by large-scale slum clearance and rehousing schemes which included the demolition of the famous Triangle as well as Rhyd-y-car. The pity is that, whilst providing better housing, such schemes of necessity destroy communities that have survived intact and in unbroken succession since the workers of the Industrial Revolution who put the Great in Britain.

Life at Rhyd-y-car

Life at Rhyd-y-car remained much the same during its entire existence as a mining community. Living conditions improved only within the physical parameters provided by the houses and gardens.

The two World Wars brought employment; the Depression forced people to rely even more heavily on the community spirit. The recollections which follow cover the period from the 1920s to the 1950s, when most of the employed menfolk were still miners. Because it was separated from the town by the canal, Rhyd-y-car had grown into a close, inter-related community.

Everybody knew everybody else's business in Rhyd-y-car. You could tell who was passing up and down. You didn't have to look, you could tell their footsteps up and down the bailey. "Oh, that's So-and-So", my mother would say. It was great. My mother never locked 'er door. She went to town, she shut it behind 'er and that was it. It was more or less a family concern then. If anybody was leaving a house or if anybody died, usually a son would jump in to the house, or you know the daughter. It was passed down in generations, you know, a lot. No-one wanted to move from there an' we weren't far from the town, five minutes you were in the bottom of the town. I mean you're right out in the country, an' yet you were so near, you know.

One of the last inhabitants of Rhyd-y-car, Mrs Elizabeth Trickett, photographed in front of her home, no. 18, in 1973. With her is her daughter, Mrs Lorna Rubbery (to right), son-in-law Mr Trevor Rubbery, granddaughter Mrs Cynthia Oxley and great-grandchildren Andrew and Sarah

The miners' working day started early:

There was an old gentleman comin' around every mornin', very old … An' 'e used to come with a walkin' stick to knock 'em up to cetch the cwbs (which were) like a train but it was all wooden. An' there were seats there for 'em to sit down. An' they was stoppin' on the Castle line for all the men, the colliers to go up. An' 'e used to come around every mornin' with a walkin' stick, this old gentleman, "Cwnnwch y ddiawled! … Cwnnwch lan, nawr!" Knockin' everybody up, about 'alf past five in the mornin', for 'em to cetch the cwbs up there.

The miner's wife ensured that he had a hot breakfast before leaving, and that his lunch-box was filled. What did he have for breakfast before he left?

Well, I'll tell you the truth. My mother used to make blackcurrant jam years and years ago and make wine out of it, so my mother used to always keep it in case one of us would be ill. Give 'im a drink of this blackcurran' an' warm water on it, you know, for 'im to 'ave a drink, and porridge and many of us 'ad sop in the morning, and a piece of toast. She'd boil a big piece of 'am on the 'ob then, bricks mind, an' we 'ad the hoven this side. And they were boiling big ham bones, and then out of what was left, we'd 'ave pea soup out of it, see, by the time we come 'ome from school. And plenty vegetables in the garden.

Plenty of vegetables. Yes. And a jack. Filled the jack up with tea. Some was having water. An' then my mother'd cut the ham then an' make sandwiches for them.

At the end of the working day there would be a good meal waiting for the miner. For a typical supper there was …

Well, cabbage from the garden, and potatoes and parsnips. My mother'd make a big meal for us then. And go to Sweets the butcher then, sixpenn'orth of pork chop. We'd 'ave two big pork chops with a kidney on for sixpence. An' two big lamb chops, and we'd 'ave a pound of sausages for sixpence or sevenpence. Oh, a difference, isn't it?

On pay day there would be a special meal, something out of the ordinary:

Yes, steak and onions then, and potsh and grafi. Potsh a grafi, they used to say, the old Welsh people, didn't they. Potsh a grafi. You don't remember that, do you? They used to mash the potatoes, mash 'em they do say now don't they? We used to 'ave potsh and gravy, see. With the steak and onions. And a big cabbage from the garden. My father'd go for a cabbage to the garden.

The twenty-nine houses at Rhyd-y-car had three communal ovens to share between them, like many other streets in Merthyr.

They were bringing their own heating sticks, and they did make a little pile in the middle and they'd put coal around. Inside the oven. And then my mother was keeping the corlac (rake) in 'er back, see, and then before she'd put the bread in, she'd spread it all around with the corlac (and) scrape it all out then … And she put 'er 'and in then to see, 'cos my mother was always baking lovely, and a few used to ask, 'er, "Come and put your 'and in now, Mary Ann, to see if it's warm enough". She knew by the feeling of it, yes. So indeed, the bread was going in then now. I couldn't tell you how long, but she knew the time it was due to come out. Oh, but what beautiful bread it was! Six large loaves. And we used to wait then for us to 'ave the warm crust off of them. Lovely bread, beautiful bread. And my mother then 'ad a big spade (peel) then to pull 'em out one by one, see, and then we used to put them on the wall then. The walls was whitewashed.

A communal baking oven from Georgetown, Merthyr Tudful, re-erected by the side of the Rhyd-y-car houses

Outside. Everybody, not only my mother. They all used to put them on the wall outside for 'em to cool a bit before they'd (put them) in a lovely big clean pan in the pantry on the stone, with a big white cloth over it.

Housework was more than just preparing food for the family. In the days before the introduction of appliances such as washing machines and spin dryers the family wash would start first thing on Monday morning and lasted all day. The washing would be done outside in a wooden tub balanced on two old chairs after the water was heated in a big iron boiler.

My mother wasn't going back to bed. She was getting up at five to see my father off to work. All, most of 'em down there. You'd see a little light in all the little windows down there, ready to go to cetch the cwbs … Oh, it would practically go on all day, washing. Washing day was terrible, especially if it was raining. It was awful. You was out there rubbing. (But) you'd be that much quicker, because you could slop to your 'eart's content, you know.

The interior of the 1805 house

After washing the floor, parts of it were decorated.

Just around the edgings it used to (be done), the stoning, the pantry floor used to be done as well, just around the edge, six inches perhaps, right the way round. The stone that my mother had in the pantry, that used to be all stoned and left on.

The range, the fireplace where all the cooking was done, was regularly polished with blacklead and all the brass kept shining.

When we'd do 'em they'd shine an' everything. An' we 'ad a little brass trivet or tricks in front of the fireplace to hold the flat irons to warm. An' my mother 'ad a black-lead one. An' that was up on the bricks. An' then on the hob we 'ad our big tea-kettle. That was black-lead all, an' that was all shining, black-lead, and there was a brass top an' a brass 'andle.

Before the days of fitted carpets and even linoleum, keeping the stone floors clean took time and effort. They were scrubbed and whitened or 'stoned' by rubbing them with a hearthstone. Even the bailey or roadway outside was scrubbed.

Usually everything would come out once a week … every corner would be turned out, mind. You'd 'ave to turn out … And I mean it was quite a work of art really … 'cos everything 'ad to be moved. The places were so small. I mean, today we go round with a hoover, but then everything 'ad to be moved. You know it was real hard work. It was never done. We was always doing something. (You had to) scrub the floor, with your canvas apron, on your 'ands and knees. An' outside. We used to scrub the outside … Not all the bailey, we'd throw water over that, but in the front of the house, that used to be done an' all, religiously. As though we lived there.

Cleanliness was indeed next to godliness. So, towards the end of the week much effort went into ensuring that the house was spotless for Sunday, and that the minimum of work was needed on the Sabbath itself.

The fire-irons came back on a Friday and was cleaned on a Friday, an' they were put over on the best side. They were cleaned and covered over, an' there was nothing in the front of the fire for Saturday, until the big cleanout then was, and then they would go back then for the weekend.

As in other areas in industrial south Wales, the only main downstairs room in the house was arranged so as to perform two functions, that of living room and parlour. Here the best furniture was arranged as a

showcase down one side of the room away from the working area, and facing the door so that it would be seen first by any visitor. This was known as the 'best side'.

> We used to buy little pieces of oilcloth then, to put on the best side. Where my mother 'ad 'er chest o' drawers, an' the couch, and a table, and a lovely tablecloth on it. It's chenille it is though, mind. And of course, I used to put that on on a Sunday, an' I'll show you the big Bible, for it to prove that I'm speakin' the truth. A big Bible on the table. Facin' our front door, that was the best side. You opened our front door then, you'd see the chest o' drawers, the sofa, an' the table.

As a practical measure it was usual to cover the table legs with old stockings or purpose-made covers.

Pit-head baths were not available, and the men would come home black with coal dust and wash in a tin bath in front of the fire.

The 'best side' in the 1925 house

> And 'course, when they used to bath in the beginning, the men, they never washed their backs. It was weakening the back or something they used to say ... and you imagine that with a white shirt on. So it got in the end they had to wash their backs. But I think the old men, you know the very old men, I don't think they used to wash their backs. They used to bath so far up, and then sit in the water, and that was your lot.

> Miners we were ... using the baths by the fire, stripped to the waist, ask the wife to wash your back, and perhaps you'd be washing your back there but perhaps somebody'd come from next door but you didn't mind in those days, we were all in the same boat ... but when you think of it now conditions were dirty ... you was putting your clothes to dry on the fire-guard and they were smelling, sweaty, and then the house had to be

seen to … oh, it was a dirty job. Hard work for the women, see. But then the pithead baths came and they made all the difference.

The men worked a six-day week. Only on Sunday was there a break in the relentless routine. Those who could went to chapel, while others observed the Sabbath as best they could at home. Some cheated slightly:

My grandfather 'e used to say, "Sarah!" – only in Welsh, see – "Cera draw i'r siop now" – to fetch peppermints. 'Cause 'e used to take a little drop of brandy or somethin' before 'e'd go to Bethel Chapel on a Sunday mornin'. An' a few of them used to 'ave 'em out on the bailey we used to call it, see, 'cause they were cobbles all. An' they'd 'ave the Bibles out and they'd read.

In this Welsh-speaking community, funerals were prefaced by a prayer meeting outside the deceased's

Above, David Kenneth Davies from no. 19 Rhyd-y-car with his 'milgi'

Below, Thomas Nicholas of no. 20 Rhyd-y-car (right) and friend, with their dog outside a shed in the 1920s

door, when hymns would be sung. But Sunday was the miners' only chance to relax with their families.

Oh, big day, Sunday, yes. It was lovely down there on a Sunday. And they 'ad beautiful gardens down there. When I was small. And I remember my father's brother comin' down, and (being shown) which was the best garden. 'E was from Georgetown. So my father used to take us over then to see our garden, the roses an' all the vegetables, kidney beans an' everything.

During the Depression years the gardens at Rhyd-y-car flourished. Men with little else to do would devote much time to growing vegetables and keeping pigs and poultry. As in other areas this became such an obsession that many men when offered work would refuse, on the entirely true grounds that they were far too busy. Many men found great enjoyment in keeping pigeons and whippets, *milgis* as they were called.

My father wanted to keep pigeons, so they moved down to Rhyd-y-car. They 'ad a garden an' there

The reconstructed pigeon loft in the garden of one of the houses

was plenty of space down there. Built 'is pigeon cot top of the garden, and that was his life … Well it was all the rage at that time, pigeons, the men 'ad nothing else much to do. They were working Saturdays of course then, those days, and they went out on Saturday night. They'd a

Left, Bessie Thomas (later Trickett), born 1880, from no. 18 Rhyd-y-car
Right, Letitia Mary Thomas (later Nicholas), Bessie's sister, born 1884
Below, a street party celebrating the end of the Second World War. The second lady from the left in the back row and the one at the extreme right are sisters Bessie Trickett and Letitia Nicholas of no. 20

bit of leisure I suppose on a Sunday, and that was their life, these pigeons. And the men that weren't working, if they were on a different shift, certain shift, they would put the pigeons on, in baskets on the railway, an' they'd be sent on, Ripon an' all sorts of places. I mean, unknown places to us in those days. An' the pigeons would fly back, an' of course, it was a great thing for the men to be up on the plain as we used to call it. And they'd run there, they'd run to a certain point and whatever was in the kitty or whatever, that was their prize. Well, it was great. I mean, that was their enjoyment. Working boots and all they'd run, you know, hobnailed boots. Black, coming home from the pits in those days.
I can remember my mother saying all his pocket money went on pigeon corn and maple seeds, an'

Left, Harry Nicholas and family, who lived at no. 26

Below, Mrs Nicholas and her sons Johnny and Willie outside no. 26, photograph taken c. 1920

what have you ... I think when he died the money that was in the kitty then went for one of these, you know the old-fashioned wreaths with a glass dome on it. And there was a dove in it, you know. That was the favourite thing wasn't it, doves and lilies, horrible things ... I always thought that was a pigeon in there, not a dove.

Pigeons did not help to pay the rent, though – pigs did.

Practically every 'ouse ... were keeping their own pigs, chickens and poultry and everyone had their garden seen to ... Their wives, grandparents reared those pigs and they were down the bottom of the garden ... near the 'ouse, in front of the 'ouse really in the garden, there was a fire built against the coal 'ouse ... a lot of the women were buying pig swill and they'd go to the slaughterhouse and buy stuff there and put it there, on the fire, that and some sharp or barley meal or peelings to feed the pigs, see. I remember pig-killing day. We used to be frightened to death of Mr Simms. He used to come from Cae-draw, and we'd be on the coal 'ouse, on the corrugated sheet top of the coal 'ouse and we'd be watching 'im and the pig would be squealing like anything, and (watch the pig being killed) outside the front door, on the bailey, under the window on the bench, my mother's bench, this famous bench that was underneath the table. And 'e'd tie 'is legs, and

'e'd hang 'im up there an' we'd watch the knife coming, and we'd watch 'im coming down like that. All the innards would drop into a bath, and then 'e would turn to us with the knife, and we'd scoot. We'd be petrified. We'd be turning our heads away. We couldn't see 'alf what was going on, but we could visualise it.

The meat was sold among the neighbours.

Mrs So-and-So would want a leg of pork. "Well she can't 'ave a leg of pork this time, because she 'ad a leg of pork the last time. She'll 'ave to be satisfied with a fillet." Or even, a bit of loin, you know. I mean, they tried to be fair, because the people with the money, you know, if the fellers, if the men 'ad good jobs, they could always afford it, couldn't they? My mother made faggots and cooked them in that oven. Everybody'd come with a jug or a basin, an' they'd 'ave some of the juice an' whatever faggots they wanted.

Pigs were not the only livestock kept.

Nearly everyone had a donkey. In fact the nickname for Rhyd-y-car in Merthyr was Donkey Town. You'll know of the Donkey Tip behind where there were always lots of donkeys grazing ... Gladys from the

A group of Rhyd-y-car children on one of the local tips - notice the donkey to the left

other row and her husband used to take me around on their cart everywhere. They used to do a lot of costering and I was always with them. Do you know the way African women carry things around on their heads? Gladys did that. In fact all the people in Rhyd-y-car carried buckets or bags on their heads and sacks under their arms.

Relaxation included reading and music. Merthyr people had always been voracious readers.

Woolworth's came to Merthyr in the 1920s and they sold books that were very popular at the time. I believe the nearest library was in Dowlais. The books were maroon in colour with gilt titles. They cost sixpence and the popular authors and the classics could be had there.

By the 1950s…

There were glass-fronted china cabinets to show off the few odd valuables: glass-fronted bookcases to show off the Complete Works of Shaw or Shakespeare and the complete set of Dickens we had as a special bargain. If you were very educated and the books spilled over, you stood them up like a row of soldiers on the top of the bookcase and pinioned them together with book-ends.

Music, too, was a delight:

A blind man lived in the other row in the 1930s. He may have been blind but what a marvellous pianist he was! My father played the cornet in the colliery band and my sister and her friends played the violin and viola. Sunday night was open house and as they say on the radio, Music Night.

Roy Davies with 'milgi' outside no. 28, photograph taken in 1934/5

Others indulged in more physical recreation. Eddie Thomas, the well-known boxer, promoter and local personality, recalls that

> There were bare-fist fights on the top every Saturday night … my father used to take part in these after coming home from the army. My grandfather fought 'The Fury' in one of the best fights ever seen there. People talked about it for years afterwards.

Eddie Thomas was not the only champion boxer to come from Merthyr: others included Jimmy Wilde, Howard Winstone and Johnny Owen.

> My grandfather used to swim the length of the canal … my father used to have a ride on his back sometimes … My mother's brother married a sister of Morgan Davies, The Wern, who was the supplier of horses for the mines in the area. Morgan Davies once jumped from the bridge into the canal, going for a swim he was, and came out with a bedroom chamber on his head. They had a devil of a job getting it off him. There was a famous little weight lifter living here – he was only about 9 stone but he could lift 250lbs above his head, easy … Tommy Whisky he was called and he used to team up with Dai Jehu and called themselves the Saldo Brothers. They were incredibly strong little men and they raised a lot of money for lots of good causes in the area.

At work and at play, the people of Rhyd-y-car considered themselves different and superior to their

Mr Tom Davies, known as Saldo, professional wrestler and weight-lifter. He was married to Jane Davies of no. 17

neighbours. The displaced survivors today are unanimous in their happy recollections of life in the face of adversity. The concluding comments of this lady are entirely typical:

> Everything changed. Oh! Oh, we do 'ave chats sometimes, if we could 'ave our old time back in Rhyd-y-car! I's telling you the truth. It was lovely there! An' the gardens an' the flowers, an' every little cottage an' toilet white-limed, an' the walls all white-limed … she got a photo of it, see. But she said I shall 'ave it. An' when I shall, I'll take another photo of it, an' you shall 'ave it.

Celebrations at Rhyd-y-car: the 1937 Coronation street party on the canal bank

Re-erection and furnishing of the houses

The beginning of the re-erection process at the Museum

Re-erecting and furnishing the Rhyd-y-car houses proved to be a demanding task but the relative abundance of specific and comparative evidence, whether architectural, documentary, oral or material, proved to be a boon of inestimable benefit.

All the houses have been finished and furnished with the greatest attention to detail: much of the background evidence has been published in this book. Re-erecting and furnishing the houses to six

different periods has allowed us to show the development of both building techniques and living styles, however much constrained by the existing buildings. The houses when built were considerably better than the average for Merthyr, but by about 1850 were already being overtaken in this respect by the new terraces of coalminers' houses being built elsewhere.

THE FIRST HOUSE – 1805

Prior to the census returns for 1841 we have little detailed information about the occupants of these houses but the vast majority would have worked in the nearby iron-ore pit, and it is as the home such a family that the first house has been furnished. The young couple, from west Wales, have brought with them the country-style oak furniture given to them as wedding presents as was usual. Ventilation is almost non-existent in the house – the windows do not open – and neither is there provision for toilets: many people used the nearby slag heaps and cinder tips.

There is a pigsty at the bottom of the garden.

Exterior of the 1805 house

The interior of the 1805 house

THE SECOND HOUSE – 1855

The interior of the 1855 house

Ventilation or sanitation have still not been improved in the fifty-five-year old house, so little wonder that five people died in Rhyd-y-car in the cholera epidemics of 1849 and another one in 1854. This house, no. 18, was inhabited in 1855 by a forty-eight-year old widow, Margaret Rosser, who had been born in Carmarthenshire. In the 1841 census she is recorded as the wife of William Rosser, ironstone miner, but he had died by 1851. Mrs Rosser earned her living as a

milkwoman, delivering fresh milk around the nearby area. Her son John, aged nineteen, worked as a coal-miner, coincidentally illustrating the way that coal-mining was taking over from iron-working as Merthyr's prime industry. Mrs Rosser also had a daughter of fourteen and a son of twelve: the boy may well have worked underground like his older brother. Mrs Rosser had no room to keep lodgers although a few of her neighbours did.

THE COMMUNAL
BAKING-OVEN

All three Rhyd-y-car ovens had been demolished by
the time the houses were offered to the Museum, but
this oven from Poplar Place, Georgetown, is exactly
comparable. The stone-slab door would have been
sealed with clay or cow-dung during baking.

THE THIRD HOUSE – 1895

Interior of the 1895 house

The Rhyd-y-car houses were surrounded by railway and tram lines by this time. The Vale of Neath Railway came up the valley and crossed to the Taff Vale station, while a branch line ran to an ironstone driftmine near the old Ynys-fach ironworks. Other lines ran to cinder heaps and mine tips. It is not surprising, therefore, that the inhabitant of no. 19 in 1895 was William Richards, railway signalman, originally from St Ishmaels in Pembrokeshire. His wife, however, had been born in Merthyr as had their daughter. Their home by now has acquired sliding-sash windows and an outside toilet in the garden, shared with neighbours. The interior of the house is typically Victorian in its cluttered appearance. The bare walls are enlivened by pictures and souvenirs, while the blackleaded hearth with its many polished brass knick-knacks serves as both the functional and visual focus of the main room. The table-legs are protected from knocks and scratches by having stockings pulled over them, a feature that can also be seen in the next house, using purpose-made covers.

THE FOURTH HOUSE – 1925

Interior of the 1925 house

Because of the moral problem of re-erecting the homes of people who might still be alive or who would certainly have living relatives, the last three houses have been furnished as type-representatives rather than the homes of specific individuals. The 1925 house illustrates a typical Rhyd-y-car phenomenon of these years, the 'best side' facing the door, furnished with better-class furniture than the rest of the main room and with linoleum underfoot instead of simply flagstones and rag mats. The clock on the chest-of-drawers is for timing racing pigeons, which were housed in the loft or 'cot' at the bottom of the garden. Water has now been brought to the house: notice the tap and bowl behind the door partition, while the main room has been wallpapered. The fire surround is a cast-iron model from the Cyfarthfa works, dated 1855, and seen in many of the Rhyd-y-car houses.

THE FIFTH HOUSE – 1955

By this time water has been brought to a kitchenette in the lean-to and the marital bed has finally gone upstairs with a small bedroom for a child taking its place. Most of the older men were still employed as coal-miners, but young couples, as envisaged here, were beginning to find work in factories such as Hoover at Pentre-bach nearby. In the garden is a large shed used as a living- and work-room allowing the room in the house to be kept for best.

Above, a reconstructed Christmas scene in the 1955 house

Right, the shed used as a living- and work-room outside the 1955 house

THE SIXTH HOUSE – 1985

Interior of the 1985 house

For the 1985 house we have taken the all-too common scenario of a middle-aged couple where the man has been made redundant, and the redundancy payment has been used to improve their home. Grant-aid would have enabled them to re-roof the house with the concrete tiles which are literally changing the colour of the valleys, but here metal windows, plastic rainwater pipes and new doors have transformed the outside while the inside has been totally re-decorated and re-furnished within the constraints imposed by the old fabric. For the first time we have a clear break with the past: this house and its contents could be anywhere in Britain – or even in the whole western world.